MAMA BEAR

Mama Bear
Copyright © 2023 by Carla Atkinson.

Published in the United States of America
ISBN   Paperback: 978-1-960629-98-2
ISBN   eBook: 978-1-960629-99-9

All rights reserved. No part of this publication may be reproduced, stored in a retrieval system or transmitted in any way by any means, electronic, mechanical, photocopy, recording or otherwise without the prior permission of the author except as provided by USA copyright law.

The opinions expressed by the author are not necessarily those of ReadersMagnet, LLC.

ReadersMagnet, LLC
10620 Treena Street, Suite 230 | San Diego, California, 92131 USA
1.619. 354. 2643 | www.readersmagnet.com

Book design copyright © 2023 by ReadersMagnet, LLC. All rights reserved.

Cover design by Ericka Obando
Interior design by Don De Guzman

Written by
CARLA ATKINSON

Illustrated by
SUE COPPLE

LETTER FROM THE AUTHOR

Atkinson youth Services was a non-profit organization providing out of home care in the form of group homes and foster families. We believed in working with the whole family; as such we worked with the natural parents of the children in our care. I had been teaching Choice Theory for about three weeks to a group of parents. However, they were not getting the idea. One mother said, "I don't understand why they keep taking my kids. I never did anything wrong. "It was the men I married." I thought for a minute and then asked "If you were a Mama Bear and someone tried to hurt your children what would you do?" She puffed herself up and said, "why, I'd chase them off – if I were a bear." From that day on I began to teach "Mama Bear Choice Theory." I began to realize that what we needed was to teach this same thing to little children, so that they grow up learning the choices a parent has to make.

Aldene was a little bear who wanted to be a Mama bear.

She lost her Mama in a forest fire when she was three years old.

Friends in the forest were very good to her and everyone took care of her.

Still, she missed having her own mother.

She watched the other mothers to see what behaviors they chose.

She saw the Mama Squirrel gather food and hide it for the winter.

"I'll be sure to save food for the winter," she said.

She saw the wise Mama Owl giving her children advice.

"I'll be sure to give my children good advice," she said.

She thought the Mama Skunk was very wise to teach her children how to protect themselves.

"I will teach my children to protect themselves," she added to her list.

Just then she saw Mama Raccoon running up and down the trees, playing with her babies.

"For sure I want to play and have fun with my children," Aldene laughed...

She was amazed as the Mama Possum tucked all her children onto her back to keep them safe while they slept.

"I will be sure to keep my children safe," she noted.

She watched the Mama Deer tenderly clean her children.

"I won't forget to keep my children clean," she said.

As she watched the Mama Blue Bird gently push her baby out of the nest she understood another "Mom behavior."

"I will help my children grow up and be independent," she said to herself.

She walked by the river just as the baby beaver made a hole in the dam. Mama Beaver was so furious that he had ruined her day's work that she pushed him right off the dam....

As Baby Beaver cried, Aldene decided,

"I will find a way to teach my children without anger and violence."

She saw a large Uncle Wolf in a bad mood stalking a Baby Wolf.

Out of the bushes came the Mama Wolf ready to fight She growled at the intruder until the Baby Wolf was safely in their hole, and then she ran a circle around the bushes and jumped into the hole with Baby Wolf "I will protect my children from bad animals, even if they are part of my family," she puffed.

At night the Bat family overhead were fighting. The mom and dad were yelling and the children felt afraid. The bat children cried, "he always comes home and yells."

Aldene made a note to herself, "a good Mama Bear will choose a good Papa Bear in the first place so there will be peace in the family.

Aldene thought if she could grow up to be a Mama Bear, she would feel safe and loved again.

As she grew up, Aldene learned it was better to be happy than sad, thankful rather than sorry for herself, and to be wise, protective, encouraging, fun, safe, strong, and at the same time tender.

Aldene thanked God for the chances he gave her to learn how to be a good Mama Bear.

She understood a Good Mama makes Good choices. She grew up into a wonderful Mama Bear.

10620 Treena Street, Suite 230
San Diego, California,
CA 92131 USA
www.readersmagnet.com
1.619.354.2643
Copyright 2023. All Rights Reserved.

www.ingramcontent.com/pod-product-compliance
Lightning Source LLC
LaVergne TN
LVHW070218080526
838202LV00067B/6846